★ CRIME FILES ★

Contents

1: Story time

You won't have heard of the place I live in. It's called Faraday and it's an out of the way town, about an hour and a half's drive from Melbourne, Australia. It's the kind of place where nothing happens – except for one day which I'll never forget.

CRIME FILES

Roy Apps

ABDUCTED

illustrated by Kevin Hopgood

FRANKLIN WATTS

LONDON • SYDNEY

First published in 2007 by
Franklin Watts
338 Euston Road
London NW1 3BH

Franklin Watts Australia
Level 17/207 Kent Street
Sydney NSW 2000

A CIP catalogue record for this book
is available from the British Library.

ISBN: 978 0 7496 7053 5

Series editor: Adrian Cole
Series advisor: Prue Goodwin, Lecturer at the
National Centre for Language and Literacy, Reading
Art director and cover designer: Jonathan Hair

Cover photo by Adrian Cole

Printed in Great Britain

Franklin Watts is a division of
Hachette Children's Books.

A note from the author:
Crime Files are
gripping true stories,
but some of the events
on which they are
based have been
dramatised and edited.

There are only ten of us in the town
school and one teacher. But that day
four of the other kids were off sick,
which meant that I was the oldest one
in school.

Miss Gibbs had only been our teacher since the beginning of term and she was dead strict.

'Craig,' Miss Gibbs said to me, 'would you collect up the maths work while I get the younger ones ready for story time? And Jordanne, would you tidy up the pencils?' Jordanne was the next oldest, after me.

'Can you read us something interesting
about killer whales or aliens, Miss?'
I asked, but she ignored me as usual.
You see, she couldn't read anything
that might scare Kelsey Hannigan,
the youngest kid, who was five.
So she read us Cinderella. Again.

I was trying to see if I could manage
to fall asleep with my eyes open when
I saw an old van pull up outside.
I didn't take any notice. I thought
Kay-Lee's folks had come early for her.
Just another fifteen minutes and school
would be over for the day!

'Cinderella was dancing in the arms
of the Prince,' read Miss Gibbs, 'when
boom-boom-boom. The ballroom
clock struck midnight.'

Bang! The classroom door crashed
open behind us. Everyone jumped
and looked around.

Two men stood there. Then I noticed
one of them had a shotgun. And he
was pointing it straight at us.

2: The gunmen

'Get outside!' yelled the gunman.
'All of you!'

I sat frozen to my seat, but the younger
kids starting screaming and crying.
We couldn't escape.

'Stop it!' shouted the gunman. 'Stop it, and be quiet or I'll shoot!'

The kids stopped screaming, but the sobbing carried on.

'I mean it!' threatened the gunman.

Then Miss Gibbs stepped forward and clapped her hands.

'Right children, let's all be as quiet as mice, shall we?'

Finally the sobs turned to snivels.

Suddenly, the man pointing the gun
at us lunged forward. 'Move!' he
snarled, shoving the shotgun towards
Miss Gibbs.

Kelsey, the youngest kid, started
sobbing again.

We all trooped outside, the gun now
at Miss Gibbs's back. I took hold
of Kelsey's hot and sticky hand.
My hand was freezing.

Outside, there was no one about.
I knew there wouldn't be. At that
time of the afternoon everybody
was working on their farms.

Parked in front of the school was a
red delivery van, with its back doors
wide open. The gunman herded us all
into the van. Out of the corner of my
eye I could see his partner pinning
something on the school door. Then the
doors slammed shut, and we were left in
total darkness.

Now all the kids were crying, and even
I couldn't stop the tears welling up in
my eyes.

'It's all right everyone. We'll soon be out
of this mess,' said Miss Gibbs. 'But until
then, I'll look after you, and Craig and
Jordanne will help me.' She sounded
so calm, but I could feel her legs shaking
against mine.

The back of the van filled with the sound of the engine starting up. Then we were thrown to the back of the van as it screeched away.

We were being driven out of Faraday by a couple of armed men. And we didn't know if we would ever be coming back.

3: In the bush

We didn't drive for long, fifteen, twenty minutes, maybe. But then, you don't need to go far from Faraday to find yourself in the middle of nowhere. It could be days before anyone found us out here, I reckoned.

We skidded to a stop. The two men came round and unlocked the back doors of the van. As they opened the doors, light flooded in, and I could see we were out in the bush.

The gunman levelled his gun at us, while the other man spoke. He talked quietly, but he was none the less menacing for it.

'You can scream for all you're worth now,' he said with a sneer. 'We're far away from the nearest farm out here.'

'What do you intend to do with us?' asked Miss Gibbs, calmly.

'What do you think? We're going to hold you captive until the government pays the ransom. We left a note on the school door with our demands. One million dollars in cash to be left at the side of the State Highway, four kilometres east of Woolagong Creek by midnight.'

'And no police or else...' added his partner, pointing the gun at each of our heads in turn.

The men ripped away some bits of
cardboard they had taped over the back
windows of the van.

Underneath, the windows were protected
by metal grilles. There was no way we
could escape through the back windows,
but at least now we weren't being held
captive in complete darkness.

The men shut and locked the doors, and
we were left in silence. I peered through
the back window. The men were over by
a tree, talking and joking.

Miss Gibbs clapped her hands. 'Right children, we've nothing to worry about! As soon as the ransom is paid, we'll all be able to go home. Until then, I think we should cheer ourselves up by singing some songs.'

Little Kelsey beamed. 'Kookaburra, Miss Gibbs!' she pleaded.

'Okay,' said Miss Gibbs. 'Come along everyone. Nice, loud voices!'
'Kookaburra sits in the old gum tree.
Merry, merry king of the bush is he...'

I felt my hand being squeezed. I turned and saw Jordanne looking at me. 'Come on, Craig,' she whispered. 'We're all in this together. You've got to join in.'

But I kept my mouth shut. I didn't feel like singing. My dad reckoned a wombat had more brains than the whole of the government. Could they be trusted to organise a one million dollar ransom? I doubted it. And if the ransom wasn't paid... I didn't want to think about it.

I thought of my mum and dad, and all the other mums and dads back in Faraday. What were they doing and thinking now? I thought about my dog Rusty, and all the other animals on the farm. I thought about playing cricket, driving the tractor, watching TV and all the other things I enjoyed doing.

I didn't want to die.

4: Time to escape

Darkness fell and everything was quiet, except for Miss Gibbs who was humming a lullaby to the kids in her arms. Amazingly, all the kids were asleep, apart from Jordanne and me. There was no way I could sleep. I was too scared; too hungry.

I could just see my watch in the light of the moon. Ten o'clock passed, then eleven o'clock, then midnight came and went. The men still sat there, watching the van. After that, I must have dozed off.

The next thing I remember was Jordanne shaking my shoulder.

'Look,' she whispered.

Peering through the grille we saw the two men striding away.

'Let's give them fifteen minutes to get far enough away,' said Miss Gibbs.

That fifteen minutes seemed more like
fifteen hours. But during that time,
Miss Gibbs crawled around the van,
tapping the sides with her knuckles.

'Now's our chance. Our only chance,'
she said. 'The bottom right-hand door
panel is the weakest spot. Craig,
Jordanne, get back from the doors and
sort the children out when they wake up.'

Miss Gibbs sat on the floor, drew her knees up to her chin and kicked her feet against the bottom door panel. The sound echoed around the back of the van and woke up the kids, who started screaming.

'It's all right,' Jordanne told them, 'Miss Gibbs has a plan.'

Thump! Miss Gibbs kicked the door again. She was wearing strong boots, but there was no sign of the door giving way. She sat back to rest her legs.

'Craig and me will have a go, Miss,' said Jordanne.

Jordanne and I sat on the floor and kicked like mad at the door panel, but it wouldn't budge. We were still trapped.

'Okay, guys, one last try,' said Miss Gibbs. She gave the door an almighty thump with both of her feet. There was a metallic screech as the first rivet gave way. From then on it was easy, and in no time at all the door panel gave way. A rush of chill night air blasted into the van.

'Craig, you crawl out first and help the others out as they come,' said Miss Gibbs.

It didn't take me long to swing out through the gap where the door panel had been.

Jordanne came out next and then we helped Kelsey, Kay-Lee and all the others through the hole in the door. Finally, out came Miss Gibbs. The hole was only just big enough for her to get through.

'I'm scared, Miss,' said Kay-Lee with
a shudder.

'Well don't be,' said Miss Gibbs. 'The men
went that way,' she pointed one way
along the track. 'And we are going that
way,' she pointed the other way along
the track.

'Where does the track lead to, Miss?'
I asked.

'I don't know Craig,' she said. 'But all roads lead somewhere, that's why they are there. Come along, everybody!'

And with the older ones taking the hands of the younger ones, we began following Miss Gibbs along the track – away from the van and out into the unknown bush.

5: The long road home

The bush was full of familiar night sounds: crickets, cockatoos and dingoes. Sounds that at home wouldn't have bothered me, but out here the noise seemed eerie and menacing.

It was the longest and scariest walk I'd ever done in my life. After about half an hour, we were all tired and hungry, and the little ones weren't fit to walk another step.

'Kelsey, Craig will give you a ride on his shoulders,' said Miss Gibbs. Kelsey might only have been little, but she weighed a ton.

We carried on walking for about an hour. My legs ached. My shoulders ached. Suddenly, Miss Gibbs said, 'Look straight ahead, children.'

We did. There in front of us, a long way off, was a light. 'About twenty minutes more should do it,' said Miss Gibbs.

The light belonged to a remote
cattle station.

As we approached the gates, some dogs
started howling. The farmhouse door
flew open and the farmer strode out, a
couple of barking dogs at his heels.
When he saw us his mouth dropped
open so wide you could see where his
teeth had once been.

'Hells bells! Flora!' he called over his
shoulder. 'It's them kidnapped kids from
Faraday!' The farmer's wife gave us
some water while Miss Gibbs rang the
police and our families.

By dinner time next day, everyone was back at home.

We had that day off school, of course, which was great.

I got up on the tractor, Rusty jumped up beside me and we went for a ride around the farm.

When I came in, I asked my mum, 'Have they caught the kidnappers yet?'

Mum shook her head.

It seemed the kidnappers had got scared off and hadn't picked up the ransom. They had just driven off. There was a massive police hunt going on, but they were still out there, somewhere.

That night I kept having nightmares about the man with the gun.

The next day when I walked into the classroom, I came over all sweaty. I thought I was going to be sick. I couldn't believe we weren't going to get abducted again.

I didn't feel entirely safe until the police eventually caught the kidnappers a couple of weeks later.

The gunman was sent to prison for
seventeen years, his partner sixteen years.

I don't have so many nightmares now.
But the memory will always haunt me.
The memory of the day we were
abducted.

i: Crime Files appendix

* The ransom

The Faraday School kidnapping, as
it became known, occurred in 1972.
According to records, the government
did offer to pay the one million dollar
ransom, but that the kidnappers failed
to turn up and collect it.

* The kidnappers

The kidnappers were eventually
caught after a big police hunt.
Their names were Edwin John
Eastwood and Robert Clyde Boland.

* Movie influence

Some people think that Eastwood and
Boland got the idea for their kidnap
from watching a movie called *Dirty
Harry*. In the movie, a kidnapper takes
a bus load of school children hostage
and demands a ransom.

* Eastwood escapes

In 1976, Eastwood escaped from prison. Two months later he abducted another teacher and a group of pupils. This time he demanded a seven million dollar ransom. However, one of the hostages escaped and alerted police. Eastwood was arrested after a shootout, and sentenced to life in prison.

* Bravery rewarded

Mary Gibbs, the 20-year-old teacher who led the schoolchildren to safety, was awarded the George Medal for bravery.

ii: Word file

Abduct – another word for kidnap; when a person is taken away by force.

Bush – any area of trees and plants, especially in Australia, where there are very few houses or farms.

Cattle station – a remote farm where cattle and sheep are kept on a huge area of land.

Dingo – an Australian wild dog.

George Medal – a special award given to people in some countries for acts of bravery and courage.

Grille – a metal grid made up of bars.

Metallic – something that is metal, or related to metal.

Ransom – an amount of money that must be paid for the release of prisoners.

Rivet – a short, metal pin.

Wombat – a furry animal that lives in burrows and is found only in Australia.

iii: Crime Files weblinks

There aren't any websites directly related to the Faraday School kidnapping, but the ones below all have a crime theme.

http://www.australia.gov.au/148

This website from the Australian government links to crime-related agencies including the Australian Crime Commission and the Australian High Tech Crime Centre.

http://www.police.tas.gov.au/on-the-beat

This website outlines the duties and departments of the Tasmania Police, one of eight Australian police services. The site includes information about special operations.

http://www.fbi.gov/kids/6th12th/6th12th.htm

This website from the United States FBI (Federal Bureau of Investigation) is for older readers. It features crime stories to follow, a FBI history timeline and crime-solving games.